MOVIEMAKERS' FILM CLUB

Be a DIRECTOR OF PHOTOGRAPHY

Make Every Shot COUNT

Alix Wood

PowerKiDS press

New York

Published in 2018 by Rosen Publishing
29 East 21st Street, New York, NY 10010

CATALOGING-IN-PUBLICATION DATA

Names: Wood, Alix.
Title: Be a director of photography: make every shot count / Alix Wood.
Description: New York : PowerKids Press, 2018. | Series: Moviemakers' film club | Includes index.
Identifiers: LCCN ISBN 9781538323700 (pbk.) | ISBN 9781538322741 (library bound) | ISBN 9781538323717 (6 pack)
Subjects: LCSH: Motion pictures--Production and direction--Juvenile literature. | Video recording--Juvenile literature. | Digital cinematography--Juvenile literature.
Classification: LCC PN1994.5 W64 2018 | DDC 791.43023--dc23

Produced for Rosen Publishing by Alix Wood Books
Designed by Alix Wood
Editor: Eloise Macgregor
Editor for Rosen: Kerri O'Donnell
Series consultant: Cameron Browne

Photo credits: Cover, 1, 4 top, 6, 8, 10, 11, 12, 13, 16, 18, 21, 22 top, 24-25 background, 25 inset, 26, 27, 28 © Adobe Stock Images; 4 bottom, 19, 20, 22 bottom © Cameron Browne; 9 Shutterstock/William Perugini. 7 © Alix Wood; all other images are in the public domain

Printed in the United States of America

CPSIA compliance information: Batch # BW18PK: For further information contact Rosen Publishing, New York, New York at 1-800-542-2595.

CONTENTS

INTRODUCING THE DIRECTOR OF PHOTOGRAPHY!

You take the stage at the movie awards ceremony and start thanking your family and your dog for all their help. You've made it as a Director of Photography. But how did you get there?

A Director of Photography (DP) is the person responsible for creating the "look" of a movie. They usually manage a team of people, from the camera operators to the **grips** that move the equipment around. The DP is involved during the whole filming process. They meet with the director at the beginning of a project to plan out the shots needed for each scene. They order equipment and check out **locations** before the filming starts. They're in charge of all the camera work during the shoot, and of checking the footage at the end of each day's filming.

One of the most important parts of the DP's job is being able to work as part of a team. You need to be happy to take instructions, and give them.

A DP needs to...

- have artistic vision
- be creative
- know about cameras and lighting techniques
- understand photography
- be flexible to new ideas
- be happy to make quick decisions
- have good attention to detail
- have good color vision
- be happy working in a team
- have great communication skills when working with actors and team members
- pay attention to the crew's health and safety
- be happy to give and take instruction

Cell Phone Movie School

You don't have to buy expensive equipment to start your moviemaking career. Many people now use their **smartphone** to make movies. There are even smartphone film festivals, where you can enter your films in competitions. You can easily share your smartphone films with an online audience using sites such as YouTube. It's never been easier to become a filmmaker.

"To me, the camera is like a musical instrument. You use it to control the flow, shape, size, and colors of images."

Conrad Hall

THE RIGHT EQUIPMENT

Don't spend much money on equipment when you first start out. Most people start moviemaking using any camera that can record video. You could use a smartphone or a regular camera. You can use more professional equipment, but it is not necessary.

Useful Everyday Cameras

You can shoot and edit movies using a smartphone or tablet, such as an iPhone or an iPad.

Small "point-and-shoot" cameras can usually also shoot video. Many have a built-in zoom lens for your **close-ups** too!

DSLR cameras were designed for photography, but they are also great for video. You can add different lenses and shoot **shallow focus** shots.

It doesn't matter if you don't have the latest gear. A great camera is still a great camera even if it's not the newest version. The most important thing that you need in order to make a great film is a good idea.

Lighting

The simplest way to light your movie is using natural light. If you want, you can use cheap work lamps to light a scene. You must be very careful. Plug them into their own power outlet. Do not cover them. Lamps get very hot and might catch fire or explode. Unplug your lamps and let them cool down before you move them or store them.

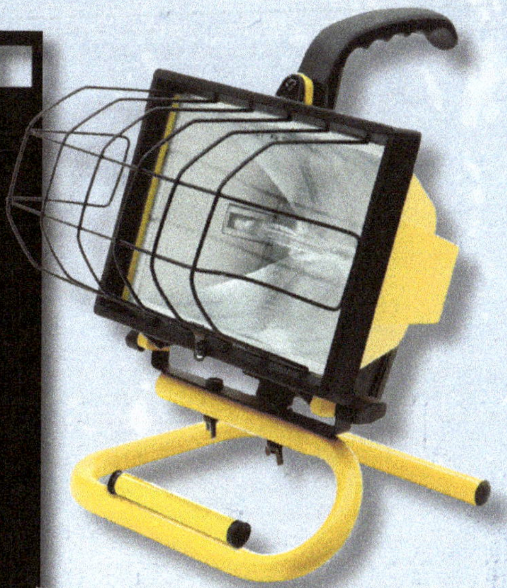

Try aiming the light from a work lamp at the ceiling. The light should bounce off the ceiling and flood the area below with a soft light.

Other Camera Equipment

A **tripod** helps keep your camera steady. You can make a simple one using string!

Get a ball of string. Tie the end into a **slipknot** around the middle of your smartphone, leaving a long end. Hold your phone at a comfortable height. Drop the ball of string onto the ground. Step on the string, keeping it taut, using one or both of your feet. Pick up the ball of string (or get a friend to, if it is out of reach). Bring the string back up to meet your slipknot end. Cut the string and tie it to the end.

To use the string tripod, hold the camera and place your foot or feet on the string. Bring the camera up until the string is taut. This will help you keep the camera at the same height as you film.

FRAMING A SHOT

Do you think a movie would look good if the camera never moved? Movies using a variety of different shots are much more interesting. Camera operators often switch between using **long shots**, **medium shots**, and close-ups. A long shot shows a person's whole body. A medium shot shows a person from the waist up. A close-up is close in on the face and shoulders, and is great for showing emotions. Using different shots can have a big effect on how the viewer sees the story.

a long shot

Using a long shot is a really useful way to show people where your scene is set. They are often used at the start of a scene.

a medium shot

a close-up

A medium shot is often used when two people are speaking. It is good for showing hand movements, too. A medium shot is the most common shot used in moviemaking.

Many camera operators use the **rule of thirds** to **frame** their shot. This rule divides a shot into nine equal parts using two imaginary **horizontal** lines and two **vertical** lines. The idea is to place important elements along these lines, or where they cross. The main reason for this is to avoid putting the subject at the center, and to prevent a **horizon** from dividing the picture in half.

Try different angles. You can shoot from the front or side, or from above. This frame of a boy and his dog is shot from below. It makes an interesting viewpoint. Camera operators may shoot from below to make the subject look big and scary.

PANS AND TILTS

To add movement to your filming, try taking **pan shots** and **tilt shots**. For a pan shot, the camera remains in a set place, but swivels around as it follows the action. For a tilt shot, the camera tilts up and down. Tilt shots are often used to bring the viewer's eye from the skyline down to the action at street level.

Pan shots are used to follow a moving character for a certain distance. The camera operator will usually position themselves around halfway between where the character starts moving and where they end up. Holding the camera at a steady height, they carefully swivel the camera as the actor walks.

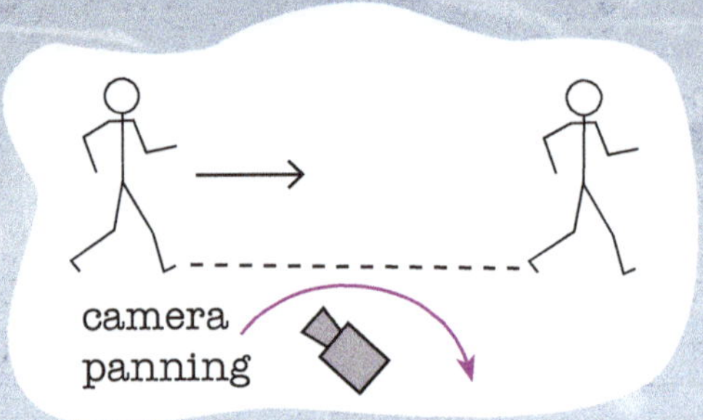

Remember the rule of thirds from page 9? If the actor is walking left to right, the camera operator will try to keep the character in the left third of the frame as they pan. This gives the actor some space to walk into.

Tilt shots can be used to follow action that is moving upward or downward. They are also often used as an **establishing shot**. An establishing shot is a wide shot that helps show where the action is taking place. An upward tilt at the start that gradually moves down to reveal more of the landscape can help build tension and give a good idea of the setting.

If you had started filming by just showing the park, you would not have established the city setting in your audience's minds.

Cell Phone Movie School

When camera operators pan using expensive film equipment, they often steady the camera using a tripod stand. To keep your smartphone panning shot steady, try pointing your feet toward where your pan shot will end. Then just turn your upper body around to face the start of the pan. As you film, move your upper body around, keeping your feet still. Using this technique makes a much smoother pan.

LINE OF ACTION

It can be quite confusing to watch a piece of action shot from different angles. Sometimes it is difficult to keep track of who is who. The "line of action" is an imaginary line between two actors. This line helps DPs stick to the **180-degree rule**. 180 degrees is half a circle. The 180-degree rule means the camera must only pan on one side of an imaginary circle around the actors, stopping at either side of the **line of action**. If DPs use the 180-degree rule, the actors won't appear to switch sides during a scene.

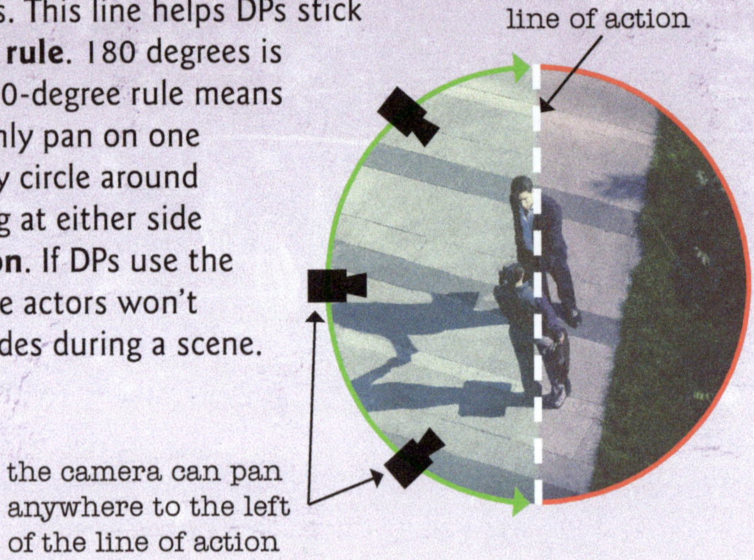

A sudden change of viewpoint can be confusing. Usually two people will stay on the same side while shooting a scene.

Of course, rules are sometimes there to be broken! Breaking the 180-degree rule is called "crossing the line." You can cross the line if you let your audience in on what you are doing. The camera could gradually move around both characters until it is on the other side of the line of action. It shouldn't be confusing if the audience was following what the camera was doing the whole time. Crossing the line is only confusing if angles chop and change suddenly with no explanation.

Cell Phone Movie School

You can't use a tripod to steady the camera as you walk around. To keep a camera as steady as possible, try holding your phone with both hands and tucking your elbows in close to your body. It also helps to get closer to the subject that you're shooting. Being far away means you have to make bigger body movements to keep things in the shot.

Don't forget to shoot some **B-roll**. B-roll is extra footage that enriches your story. Film the two boys talking, get shots of them walking around, and a close-up of them studying. You can mix these shots in when you edit.

ZOOMING, DOLLYING, AND TRACKING

The Director of Photography can move the camera forward and backward in a few different ways. Your camera may be able to zoom, or focus in closer to your subject. Here are some of the filming techniques you can try.

Zooming
Making the subject appear closer or further away by changing the focal length of the lens.

Dollying
Moving toward or away from the subject. To "dolly-in" is to move toward the subject, and "dolly-out" is to move back. A dolly is a wheeled platform the camera sits on, sometimes placed on tracks. The term "dollying" is still used for moving in and out even if the camera is handheld.

Tracking
Moving left or right. Unlike panning, the camera stays pointing straight ahead, but is physically moved to the left or right. Tracking shots are often used when filming someone walking along.

Cell Phone Movie School

When zooming using a smartphone, it is best not to use the phone's digital zoom. Digital zoom stretches the **pixels** and results in poor quality images. It is better to move the phone closer to the subject instead.

Movies can be made by a team of 2 to 70 people. On a big film set, grips help the camera department. They build and look after any equipment that holds the cameras. In a small crew, a grip's tasks may be done by the DP. Grips will usually push the dolly during filming.

A dolly grip's job is to guide the camera operator. They even have to physically guide them if the operator is walking using a handheld camera. The operator is too busy concentrating on the camera to see where they are going. The dolly grip will silently push, pull, and nudge the operator along so they don't trip or crash into anything!

"If I were ever stranded on a desert island there would be three things I'd need: food, shelter, and a grip."

George C. Scott

LOW AND HIGH ANGLES

Different camera angles can make scenes look much more dramatic. The angle that the Director of Photography decides to shoot a character from affects how the audience thinks about them. If a character is to appear strong they might shoot them from a low angle. A weak character is more likely to be looked down at from a high angle.

Sometimes a movie's main character starts off weak and gradually grows in strength as the story unfolds. A great way of subtly showing this journey is to start the movie shooting slightly higher than eye level. As the character becomes more sure of themselves the angle lowers to eye level and then drops to below eye level as they become even more courageous.

low-angle shot

high-angle shot

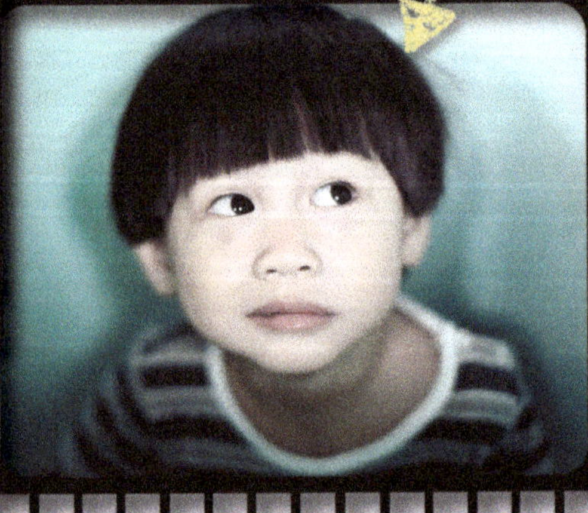

The background of a low angle shot is often just sky or ceiling.

Cell Phone Movie School

When you shoot a landscape, make sure your horizon is level. It looks pretty weird to have sea that is leaning uphill! Remember your rule of thirds, too. Have your horizon run along one of the two imaginary horizontal lines. Either shoot from a low angle so it runs along the top line or from a higher angle so the horizon is along the bottom line.

Shooting from eye level is the most common angle. This angle is how we see the world on a daily basis. It has no dramatic power itself. It is good to use when we want to see the subject on equal terms.

A **pedestal shot** moves the entire camera up or down without tilting the lens. You might want to use a shot like this if you are showing how tall someone is. Start filming at the feet and then gradually lift the camera up until you reach their head. You could also use a pedestal shot to follow someone who is climbing a wall.

CRANES AND DRONES

On a big-budget movie, a DP can get an even higher angle shot by mounting a camera to a crane or a drone. Aerial shots like these are often used as establishing shots. Establishing shots are shots of the building or landscape where the action will be set. They are usually used at the beginning of a movie, or scene, to establish where the characters are.

Crane shots are a good way to make people seem insignificant or a small part of a larger world. This idea might work with your story line. How does your character fit into their community?

"When you ... do a shot like the crane down ... then it's got to mean something. You've got to know why you're doing it; it's got to be for a reason within the story."

Roger Deakins

A **top shot** looks down on the action from overhead. It is sometimes known as the "God shot" or "bird's-eye view." It can be used to show a battle, or perhaps a crowded city. The angle can make familiar objects unrecognizable at first. A DP might zoom in on a drop of rain falling on some fabric and gradually pull back until it becomes obvious it is a crowd holding umbrellas on a rainy day.

Cell Phone Movie School

You can get a similar effect to a drone or crane shot by shooting your scene from a high vantage point. Try shooting the action from an upper window, a hill, or a safe wall or ledge.

In this student film, part of the action was filmed by a camera operator sitting on a wall. In this picture, the DP is discussing the shot with the crew while the actors wait.

LIGHTING THE SHOTS

If the natural light available isn't what you want, you may have to make some artificial light. Filmmakers traditionally use three lights.

- a main **key light**, in front and a little to one side of the subject
- a **fill light**, on the opposite side of the key light and about half as bright. This light helps to soften the shadows.
- a **rim light** behind the subject, to make the edge of the subject stand out from the background.

You can use some natural light as one of your light sources. Perhaps use light from a window as your key light.

Make your lighting consistent. A long scene may mean shooting at the same location from morning through to night. You need to make sure the lighting is the same during all the filming, otherwise it will look weird. That's why professional filmmakers usually don't rely on natural light, as it may change.

If two shots in the same scene were lit this differently, it would look jarring.

Direct sunlight and bare lightbulbs can cast unwanted hard shadows. Your images will look better if you can soften or reduce shadows. Try using a white umbrella as a simple reflector. Place the open umbrella so the inside is pointing at your subject. Then shine your light toward the inside of the umbrella. The umbrella will reflect a nice, soft light back onto the subject.

It is worth getting your lighting right while you film your movie. It can be hard to improve badly lit images later.

Cell Phone Movie School

Try making your own reflector board by covering a sheet of foam core board with aluminum foil. You could make two reflectors, one using the shiny side and another using the duller side. They both will give different light effects. For another effect, try scrunching the foil first before smoothing it out and covering the board. The small crinkles help bounce the light around even more. Plain foam core board gives a nice soft light, too.

SHOOTING INSIDE

Shooting a movie scene indoors has its own challenges. The room might be very tight for space. It's not unusual for the camera operator to be pressed against a wall and the sound person to be hanging onto a curtain rail.

Your team may have a Location Manager who scouts out places to film your movie. The Director of Photography should always check out a location, too, though.

The DP should check where windows and other sources of daylight are, and if there are any lights that would be useful. They also need to check which direction the location is facing. That will warn them if the sun might suddenly stream through a window at some point in the day.

Cramped locations may mean the Director of Photography works squashed in a cupboard!

Lighting Indoor Shots

- It is usually easier to artificially light an indoor location than an outdoor one. You might be able to use ceiling lights and lamps that are already there, known in the trade as "practicals."
- You can use the walls as a giant reflector. Point a work lamp at a wall or ceiling and the light will bounce back. Pale walls are best for this. A brightly colored wall will reflect its color onto the subject.
- Use work lamps to light from the side for close-ups.
- Chinese paper lanterns with bright low-energy bulbs can give a nice, soft lighting effect.

To control the light when filming indoors, it is a good idea to black out all the windows. Tape black drapes or trash bags to the glass. Don't tape to the frame as it might pull off any paint. Light will get through even tiny gaps, so make sure the tape goes all the way to the edges. Go inside to double check your black-out is good enough. It is hard to tell from the outside.

You can also cover your windows with aluminum foil if they won't be in the shot. Spray the window with water and then roll the foil over it. It will stick.

SHOOTING OUTSIDE

There are many more challenges for the DP when shooting outdoors. The weather can be very unpredictable.

Rain

Imagine you have shot half a scene in bright sunlight, and then it starts to rain. To stop unexpected rain affecting how a scene will look, a DP may ask for the set to be "wetted down" at the beginning of filming. If the set is wet from the start, a sudden downpour won't affect the **continuity**.

Sun

Sun can be awkward too! Your "Key light" moves around and up and down throughout the day, and you have no control over where and when it moves. The color of the light changes, too, at different times of day. A sunset may glow red. The length and direction of shadows also change. Sudden haze or cloud will also affect how the scene looks. A DP should check locations with the Sun in mind. They can then figure out where it will be at different times of day and plan out which scenes to shoot at what time.

Wind

One of the main problems with wind is that it can blow your equipment over! Also, the actors' hair and clothes will move around. Sometimes, a well-placed screen can block out the wind and you can continue to shoot your movie.

Cell Phone Movie School

When you are making a cell phone movie, if you can, choose a day with even cloud cover. If you have to film in strong sunlight, try to shoot from as high up as possible. This will help keep the sky from being in the frame. Too much light can overwhelm a cheap camera. By shooting from up high, the camera will adjust to the subject you are filming, and not focus on the overly bright sunlight.

Backlighting—that is, having your light source behind the action—makes the foreground objects **silhouetted**. Try it by placing your subject between you and the setting sun.

"Every shot I have ever made has been a compromise in some way. No image has ever been as good as the one I envisioned in my mind's eye."

Conrad Hall

FOCUSING YOUR SHOTS

Getting your shots in **focus** is usually done by the camera assistant. "In focus" means an image that is sharp and clear. But which part of the shot should be in focus? All of it? Some of it? The foreground? The background? These are all choices a DP can make to create a more interesting movie.

People in moviemaking talk about the **depth of field**. The depth of field is the distance between the nearest and farthest objects in a shot that are in sharp focus.

When the distance between the nearest and farthest objects in focus is very large, that is known as **deep focus**. The foreground, middle ground, and background are all in focus. Deep focus is great for filming a landscape, as everything is clear.

This shot is in deep focus. You can clearly see the objects in the foreground and background.

The closer you are to your subject, the shallower your focus will be. Move back if you want a deep focus.

When the distance between the nearest and farthest objects in focus is very small, it is known as shallow focus. Shallow focus is good to use when you want something to stand out from its background.

In this shallow focus image, the blue post stands out the most, as the other posts are out of focus.

Cell Phone Movie School

Smartphones usually focus automatically. Automatic focus generally gives deep focus, and works best in good light. In low light, it is best if you focus the camera yourself. You can usually force a smartphone to focus by tapping on the screen on the area you wish to focus on. Different phones work in different ways, so read your phone's instructions.

Focusing a regular digital camera

If you use a DSLR or a point-and-shoot camera, look for a menu containing pictures of a mountain and a person's head. Selecting the mountain gives you a deep focus suitable for landscapes. Selecting the head gives you a shallow focus suitable for portraits.

LENSES AND FILTERS

Sometimes a DP might want to bring the action closer, or add a rosy glow to their shots. Different types of lenses can help change the focus of a shot. Filters help **enhance** the color or cut glare.

Prime Lenses

A prime lens **simulates** how the human eye sees. It won't do fancy zooming, but it costs less, too. Moviemakers have used prime lenses for over a century. They record sharp images and are good for filming in low light.

Wide-angle Lenses

A wide-angle lens is used for filming a landscape, as it captures more width than a prime lens. It is useful in a cramped space, too. If walls keep you from backing up enough to fit everything in a shot, a wide angle lens will help. They can **distort** an image, however. Straight lines may appear bent.

Cell Phone Movie School

Wide is good. Never film a smartphone movie holding the camera vertically. Screens are horizontal, so the footage will look odd when you view it later. Always hold your phone horizontally and get a nice, wide shot.

Zoom Lenses

A zoom lens allows you to change the focal length, so you can focus on things nearby or far away by adjusting the lens. They are great if you can't stop to change a lens. If you need just one lens for every occasion, get a nice zoom lens.

Telephoto Lenses

A telephoto lens helps bring faraway objects closer. These are particularly useful when filming something dangerous, like a dangerous car stunt, or a lion in the wild. You can be a long way away and still get a close-up shot.

It would probably be best to use a telephoto lens when filming this guy!

Using Color Filters

Color-balancing filters attach to a lens to add a color effect to your filming. Use them to warm up or cool down your "look."

- Use warm filters such as pink or gold when filming a romantic scene. The color tends to make a viewer feel happy.
- Use cool colors such as blue and gray to create a somber mood. A movie set in a prison might be shot using blue or gray filters.
- A green filter would give the scene a spring-fresh look, which would work well when filming a countryside setting.

GLOSSARY

180-degree rule A rule which states the camera should stay on one side of the action.

B-roll Extra footage filmed to enrich the story.

close-ups Film images taken at close range and showing the subject on a large scale.

continuity Consistency of details in the various scenes of a film.

deep focus Where foreground, middle ground, and background objects are all in focus.

depth of field The distance between the nearest and the furthest objects that are in focus.

distort Pull or twist out of shape.

dollying Moving a camera forward or backward on a mobile platform.

enhance Improve the quality.

establishing shot Usually the first shot of a new scene, to show where the action is taking place.

fill light A light used chiefly to lighten shadows.

focus To adjust a camera so that the image is sharp and clear.

frame One picture of the series on a length of film.

grips Members of the camera crew who set up, move, build, and maintain equipment.

horizon The line at which the Earth's surface and the sky appear to meet.

horizontal Parallel to the horizon.

key light The main source of light in a photograph or film.

line of action An imaginary line drawn between the two actors.

locations Places away from a studio where a movie is shot.

long shots Views of a scene shot from a considerable distance.

medium shots Camera shots in which the subject is in the middle distance.

pan shot Moving the camera horizontally so that it sweeps around the scene.

pedestal shot Moving the camera up or down without changing its vertical or horizontal axis.

pixels The basic unit of programmable color on a computer or TV screen.

rim light Backlighting used to create the appearance of a halo of light.

rule of thirds A photography technique where images are divided into thirds by two imaginary horizontal and vertical lines.

shallow focus The opposite of deep focus, where only one plane is in sharp focus.

silhouetted A dark shape outlined against a brighter background.

simulates Imitates the appearance or character of something else.

slipknot A knot that can be undone by a pull.

smartphone A cell phone that can be used to send and receive e-mail, connect to the Internet, take photographs, etc.

tilt shot Where the camera stays in a fixed position but rotates up and down in a vertical plane.

top shots Shots that look directly down on a scene, not at an angle.

tracking The camera moves alongside the object it is recording.

tripod A three-legged stand for supporting a camera.

vertical At right angles to a horizontal plane.

zooming Changing the distance between the camera and the object being filmed by using a zoom lens.

FOR MORE INFORMATION

Books

Blofield, Robert. *How to Make a Movie in 10 Easy Lessons: Learn How to Write, Direct, and Edit Your Own Film Without a Hollywood Budget (Super Skills)*, Lake Forest, CA: Walter Foster Jr., 2015.

Stoller, Bryan Michael. *Smartphone Movie Maker*. Somerville, MA: Candlewick, 2017.

Websites

Due to the changing nature of Internet links, PowerKids Press has developed an online list of websites related to the subject of this book. This site is updated regularly. Please use this link to access the list:

www.powerkidslinks.com/mm/Photo

INDEX